NICOLE B. ADAMS

Running with God

A Devotional Journey Through the Race of Faith

First published by Nicole B. Adams Publishing 2026

First edition

ISBN: 979-8-9950565-0-8

This book was professionally typeset on Reedsy.
Find out more at reedsy.com

For my mom,
whose life was a race lived in sacrificial love.

Contents

How to Use This Devotional

This devotional is not meant to be rushed or completed according to a rigid schedule. Like running with God, it is meant to be intentional, reflective, and personal—and journaling is a central part of that process.

Each chapter is designed to be read at a pace that fits your current season of life. Some readers may choose to read one chapter a day, while others may take several days with a single chapter—reading, reflecting, praying, and writing as they go. There is no "right" way to move through this book. What matters most is creating space to meet with God honestly and attentively.

Journaling is strongly encouraged as you work through this devotional. Writing helps slow us down, clarify what God is revealing, and notice patterns in our thoughts, prayers, and growth over time. You may choose to journal freely, respond to specific questions, write prayers, or record moments where Scripture or a story stands out to you. There is no expectation of polished writing—this is simply a place to be real with God.

Throughout the chapters, you will find personal stories, Scripture, and reflections meant to help connect the physical act of running with the spiritual journey of faith. When something resonates, pause. Write about it. Ask God what He may be inviting you to notice, release, or trust more deeply.

At the end of each chapter, you will find reflection questions and a prayer. These are not meant to test your understanding, but to prompt deeper awareness and conversation with God. You do not need to answer every question. Sometimes one question is enough to guide a meaningful journaling time.

This devotional can be used individually or in a small group setting. If you are reading with others, consider sharing insights from your journaling—what surprised you, challenged you, or encouraged you. Hearing how God is working in different lives reminds us that this race of faith is not meant to be run alone.

Above all, approach this devotional with grace—for yourself and for the process. Some days your journaling may flow easily; other days it may feel quiet or unfinished. God meets you in both. Keep showing up, keep writing, keep listening, and trust that He is running with you every step of the way.

Introduction – Entering the Race

"Therefore, since we are surrounded by such a great cloud of witnesses, let us throw off everything that hinders and the sin that so easily entangles, and let us run with perseverance the race marked out for us." (Hebrews 12:1, NIV)

This book is not just for people who love to run. It is a journey every Christian is called to walk with intention. And honestly, it isn't about running in a literal way. While Scripture uses the language of a race, it most often refers not to a physical run, but to a mental and spiritual one. The image of a race reminds us that faith is not something we simply believe—it is something we live, moving forward with purpose even when the path is difficult. The things we will discuss—pace, the course, and the finish line—have literal examples, but we will explore them through a spiritual lens. Many, if not all, of the illustrations in this book come from real, physical experiences, with the hope that they help you better understand and apply truth to your own spiritual race.

As we walk through this race of faith together, we will explore pace and preparation, community, obstacles, healing, and what it means to finish well. My hope is that through the physical illustrations I have experienced, you will see spiritual truths woven throughout the race. Most importantly, I invite you to slow your pace as you read, allowing space for reflection and for God to speak personally and intentionally into your life. While the world rewards the fastest runner, God rewards the one who remains in the race with Him. So, let's get running.

While many pursuits require specialized skill or strength, running does not. Even people with disabilities can run. It may not look the way we expect, but they are still choosing to move forward. Faith is the same. God doesn't want us to wait until we have read the entire Bible or memorized a certain number of Scriptures. He equips us where we are right now to run the race He has set before us, and He will provide what is needed along the way.

I started running as a kid, like most kids do. I ran when we played tag, trying to escape the person who was "it." As I got into high school, I began to take running more seriously. I ran for sport and discovered that when I applied myself, I was capable of more than I imagined. However, I was often lazy and didn't always do my best. Now, as an adult, I run for fun. Okay, do I really enjoy it? Not all the time! Sometimes it is hard. Sometimes I am tired and don't want to go. I do it for the benefits I gain from it. Our walk of faith can be the same. We know it is beneficial and necessary, yet without intention and perseverance, we often approach it half-heartedly instead of running with purpose.

Later in life, I began running again because I wanted to lose weight, but I quickly discovered it was also a time when God would speak into my life. I use that phrase intentionally. It isn't God speaking to me about general things; it is a time when He speaks specific life lessons to me. There is freedom in that. I don't have to get discouraged when I'm not seeing the results I expected. It is my time with God, and that can never disappoint.

When I reflected on Hebrews 12:1, I realized that my physical struggle on the pavement mirrored a spiritual reality. God uses the image of a race because faith, like running, is not a stagnant state—it is forward motion. It requires us to strip off the "extra weight" that slows our souls down.

I also realized that the race God describes in His Word isn't about my own effort or speed; it's about a different kind of application.

This book isn't about running a solo race to impress Him. It's about running with Him. To run with God means matching our stride to His. It is the daily practice of checking our spiritual pace against His Word, ensuring we aren't gasping for breath because we've tried to outrun His grace, nor sitting on the sidelines because we've lost heart.

As Christians, it's important to recognize the call to run with God. While the destination is heaven, what happens in the interim matters—not only for us, but for others as well. It's like sitting on a highway with the destination clearly ahead, yet never moving toward it. Running with Him is understanding how faith plays out in daily life. We will explore why this matters in the coming chapters.

Even if your "race" looks more like time in a garden, the principles of pace, breath, and endurance remain the same. It becomes a time when we draw close to Him. We all need something in our lives that pulls us away from the noise of the world and helps us focus on our time with God—somewhere or something that allows for fewer interruptions. My runs aren't always distraction-free, but for the most part my kids aren't running after me with questions, my dog isn't asking to be fed, and life is quieter. Whatever that looks like for you, make the decision to commit to this race.

Running with God is intentional communion. It's not just about the destination; it's about the day-to-day, breath-to-breath conversation with the Creator while you are in motion.

Put these truths into practice so you can run the way you were meant to. Let's begin by exploring why we were created to run this race.

1

Why Run? - Training the Body and Spirit

"Physical training is good, but training for godliness is much better, promising benefits in this life and in the life to come." (1 Timothy 4:8, NLT)

I didn't start running because I loved it. I started because something needed to change. Some mornings, my legs felt heavy before I even began, and my mind was already focused on how far I still had to go. When I fixed my attention on the discomfort, the run felt endless.

But something shifted when I stopped running alone. When I began inviting Jesus into that time- talking with Him instead of listening to my own complaints- the run didn't suddenly become easy, but it did become lighter. The struggle didn't disappear, but it no longer defined the experience. What began as physical movement slowly became a place of listening, trust, and learning to keep going.

That question- *why run with God*-began to surface as I paid closer attention to what was truly motivating me.

Why run with God? God has created each one of us with an innate desire for relationship with Him. "He has also set eternity in the human heart" (Ecclesiastes 3:11, NIV). I believe this longing shows up in our drive to achieve and in our desire for more. Even beyond our basic needs, we are driven to pursue something greater.

Many times, those who are especially driven are labeled as having a Type A personality. Whatever they have never feels like enough. If they earn a bachelor's degree, they want a master's degree. If they have a fast car, they want a faster one. If they have a good job, they want a better job. I'm not suggesting that human drive is the sole reason for this longing, but it certainly contributes- especially in a culture that constantly pushes us toward bigger, better, and more.

This drive is rooted in something deeper than we often realize. Often, we do not experience the contentment and fulfillment in God that He created us for. We feel a strong desire but do not always recognize it for what it truly is. I can physically feel it at times. Many of us are deeply aware of our emotions, and that awareness can both help and hinder us as we run.

It is that longing I feel in my chest when I deeply desire something. It may be the tightness I feel as I think about being with someone I miss, or the strong hope that rises as I pray for someone's healing. It can also be the heaviness in my heart when I long for a marriage to be restored.

Do we long for Him that way? I do. I want more. Do you feel it too? When we experience that longing, it is because God has placed it within us. He wants us to turn to Him. He created that desire so that we would seek the same relationship with Him that He desires to have with us. More often than not, we fail to recognize this longing as something only God can satisfy, and we attempt to fill it with something else altogether. Usually, it is something tangible- but in the end, it remains worldly and temporary. As humans, we are always seeking more. Without God, there is a void, and we try to fill it with substitutes. Scripture warns us that when we attempt to satisfy our deepest longings apart from Him, we are easily led astray. Proverbs 3:1-2 reminds us, *"My child, never forget the things I have taught you. Store my commands in your heart. If you do this, you will live many years, and your life will be satisfying."* (NLT)

This isn't just a struggle for those who don't know God. Even those who have a relationship with Him can continue to wrestle with fulfillment and contentment. We are still human, and Scripture says, *"Human desires are like the world of the dead- there is always room for more"* (Proverbs 27:20, GNT). We will not experience true fulfillment or contentment unless we are living in the relationship with God that He desires for us. I believe that when you are where He wants you to be, you will know it. And when we are right where He wants us, we can find peace and joy in all circumstances.

* * *

Reflection & Prayer

1. Where do I notice a persistent desire for "more" in my life right now?
2. In what ways have I tried to fill that longing with things other than God?
3. When have I experienced true contentment or peace in my relationship with Him?
4. What distractions or ambitions most often pull my focus away from God?
5. What would it look like to intentionally pursue a deeper relationship with Him in this season?

Father God, place within me a deeper desire for You alone. Help me recognize when I am chasing fulfillment apart from You. Draw my heart toward the life You created me to live—fully surrendered and fully alive. Teach me to run this race with purpose and faith. Amen.

* * *

2

Preparation - Fueling, Equipping, and Readying the Heart

"Do you not know that your body is a temple of the Holy Spirit, who is in you, whom you have received from God? You are not your own."
(1 Corinthians 6:19, NIV)

Preparation

I didn't begin running with spiritual training in mind. I started because I wanted to lose weight. We have all heard the reports explaining why maintaining a healthy weight is so important, and we know the health benefits are extensive. Exercise strengthens our hearts, supports a healthy metabolism, lowers blood pressure, and reduces strain on our joints, bones, lungs, and heart.

Running well doesn't begin on the course; it begins with preparation-both physical and spiritual.

But what about our spiritual walk? Why should we walk with God? What are the benefits to our lives?

What does obedience to God actually offer us? We can accept Jesus as our Lord and Savior and assume the work is done- after all, we know we are going to heaven.

I'm not implying that we are all meant to be in top physical form or run a marathon. However, it is important to do the best we can to care for our bodies and to remain open to the Holy Spirit's prompting in the areas of our health and well-being.

Scripture reminds us that we do not live by bread alone, but by every word that comes from God (Deuteronomy 8:3; Matthew 4:4). Our strength ultimately comes from Him- not from our own effort. Yet dependence on God is not the same as neglecting stewardship. God often works through our preparation rather than around it.

My heart was in the run that day, but my body was not.

It was a Monday morning, and I had eaten poorly all weekend. You would think that when you eat a lot of fat, your body would cooperate when you try to burn it off- but instead, I was dragging. It felt as if all that heaviness had settled in the soles of my feet, making it hard to move forward.

When I ran track in high school, my mom used to make pasta for me the night before a meet. I was told that the stored carbohydrates from the pasta would help give me energy the next day when I ran my events. I don't know if that still holds true today- or if research has shown something else to be more beneficial- but I do know this: what you eat affects your run, and what you don't eat affects it as well. Sometimes proper nutrition, even from the day before, can provide the energy needed to keep going. In the morning, something as simple as a banana or a piece of toast helps me. And of course, water is essential. Anytime we push our bodies and begin to sweat, we lose fluids. Because our bodies are made up largely of water, staying hydrated is critical. When we become dehydrated, our bodies quickly begin to fail.

Our spiritual walk is much the same. If we do not have the Bread of Life and the living water in our lives daily, our spirit will begin to grow weak and falter.

Have you ever noticed that we don't fully realize our need for these things until we are desperate for them? We get hungry and eat, or thirsty and drink. But think about air. It isn't until we are desperate for it- until we can't breathe- that we truly understand how much we need it. What would it look like to seek God with the same urgency we feel for food, water, and our next breath?

I have to eat breakfast before I run, or I don't have the energy to make it around the lake. I usually have a piece of toast- bread. When we are finished, we need to refresh ourselves, because we have lost fluids. In the same way, we need to fill ourselves with living water. We must continue in Him through His Word and through prayer.

We need to continue nourishing ourselves so that we can remain strong in Him.

How we prepare our bodies and spirits matters- not so that we can perform better, but so that we are ready to respond when God asks us to move.

Preparation doesn't always mean starting strong; sometimes it means starting gently.

Warming Up

"Everything that was written in the past was written to teach us, so that through the endurance taught in the Scriptures and the encouragement they provide we might have hope." (Romans 15:4, NIV)

Sometimes we need to get back on track- or perhaps we were never on track to begin with. We may be just beginning our walk of faith, or we may have wandered so far from it that we need to find our way back. Let's face it: you can't always start running. Sometimes you need to warm up again.

What do we do when we aren't sure where to begin? We can't allow our fear of not knowing where to start to keep us from taking the first step. We must become familiar with the One we are going to run with. If I run with my husband, whose stride is longer than mine, I may need to slow down to make the distance- or lengthen my stride to keep up. If I run with a friend whose stride is shorter, I must adjust as well. In the same way, we need to know the God we are running with so we can keep pace with Him and understand what He is asking of us in our run.

There are two important things that even the most experienced Christians often forget or overlook. We can only truly know someone if we spend time with them. When we spend time with God, we come to know Him in two essential ways. There are many ways to know God, but if we neglect these two, we can easily miss the foundation of that relationship. It is the difference between knowing someone as an acquaintance and knowing them as a friend. We must seek to know God intimately through reading His Word and through prayer, and it is vital that we do this daily.

My husband and I are a good example of this. When we first got married, we had different ways of doing things, different goals, and different schedules. As we grew together in marriage, we each had to adjust our thoughts, ideas, and plans to make the relationship work. The difference, however, is that in our relationship with God- because He and His plans are perfect- we must always be the ones willing to adjust to Him.

As my husband and I spent more of our lives together, our marriage began to move in greater harmony- imperfect as we are- but I could not truly know him apart from living life with him day by day. We come to know God in much the same way: through daily prayer and time in His Word.

It is possible to run without warming up. Many experienced runners can start running right away if they choose- but most do not. Warming up is not difficult. It is simple, doesn't require much effort, and helps protect us from injury. You may be wondering how this relates to our Christian run. There are certain practices that are important in the life of a believer. They are often referred to as disciplines, though people may disagree about which ones belong on that list. One thing that cannot be disputed is believing in Jesus as our Lord and Savior. Other important steps include baptism and spending time in God's Word, as we have already seen.

Just as it wouldn't be advisable to run without warming up, it wouldn't be wise to run with God without a prayer life. In fact, prayer must be more than a daily routine- it should be woven into our thoughts and our breath. We are meant to be in ongoing conversation with God throughout the day. More specifically, what I want to focus on here is morning prayer- the prayer that begins our day and sets a tone that acknowledges God's presence and authority in our lives.

It is possible to run without warming up, just as it is possible to walk without prayer- but neither is advisable.

"Surely you know that many runners take part in a race, but only one of them wins the prize. Run, then, in such a way as to win the prize. Every athlete in training submits to strict discipline, in order to be crowned with a wreath that will not last; but we do it for one that will last forever." (1 Corinthians 9:24-25, GNT)

It can feel like a contradiction when Jesus says that those who eat and drink what He gives will be satisfied and never hunger or thirst again - when I experience Him, I always want more. I can never seem to get enough. While He is speaking of spiritual nourishment, our physical needs are also met as we accept Him and continue to seek Him- not just met, but satisfied. When our physical needs are satisfied, we are better able to focus on our spiritual needs and our relationship with Him. And in that relationship, we will always desire more of Him. He designed it that way so we would continue to seek Him. What we receive spiritually is deeply satisfying, yet so good that it awakens an even greater hunger. When you taste something truly good, you don't want to stop- you want more.

* * *

Reflection & Prayer

1. What habits currently prepare me to walk closely with God? Which ones weaken me?
2. What areas of my life feel undernourished—physically, spiritually, or emotionally?
3. How intentional am I about daily time in God's Word and prayer?
4. What might God be inviting me to adjust so I can run with greater strength and endurance?
5. Where do I need to slow down and "warm up" rather than rush ahead?

Father God, thank You for caring about every part of who I am—body, mind, and spirit. Help me prepare well, not out of fear or obligation, but out of love and trust in You. Teach me to nourish my life daily through Your Word and prayer, and to care for the body You have entrusted to me. When I feel weak or unprepared, remind me that You are my strength. I want to run this race faithfully, with a heart ready for whatever You call me to. Amen.

* * *

3

Keeping Pace - Staying in Step with Christ and Others

"For the pagans run after all these things and your heavenly Father knows that you need them. But seek first his kingdom and his righteousness, and all these things will be given to you as well. Therefore do not worry about tomorrow, for tomorrow will worry about itself. Each day has enough trouble of its own." (Matthew 6:32-34, NLT)

Keeping Pace with Christ

Part of learning to run with someone is paying attention to where they are in relation to you. As I began thinking about running with Jesus, I realized I was considering details I had never thought about before. When you run with someone, they are usually beside you- so I found myself wondering which side Jesus would be on.

What I was really wrestling with wasn't position, but proximity- how closely I was paying attention to Him.

I had to think about it intentionally. At first, I envisioned it incorrectly and placed Him on my right. We often hear about the right hand of

God. But if Jesus is at the right hand of God, then we would be at Jesus' right hand- which would place Him on our left.

One morning I was running and had just started my first lap. I was really feeling good that day. As I turned the second cul-de-sac, one of my neighbors saw me and began walking toward me. I silently prayed that she wouldn't stop to talk- but of course she did, about things that weren't important and could have waited. Once I stopped, it was very difficult to get started again. It had only been a few brief minutes, but at that point my body- or my mind- decided it was done. I did manage to run a few more laps, but it was a struggle.

"Yet I am always with you; you hold me by my right hand." (Psalm 73:23, NIV)

It is easy for us to become focused on other things. We can allow finances, relationships, jobs, and responsibilities to pull our attention away from Christ. These are the things of the world that can consume us, and our society often tells us they are the most important priorities in our lives.

When you are tired and weary, sometimes He will move ahead of you. Keep your eyes on Him, and try not to lose sight of where He is leading. At times, He may continue forward while we hesitate, inviting others to take part in what He has planned. That is why it is so important to remain attentive and keep Him in view.

Even good relationships- those that are healthy and true blessings from God- can sometimes draw our eyes away from Him. When that happens, we risk allowing good gifts to take the place that only God should hold.

There was a time in my life when I realized this in my own marriage. I have no doubt that my husband is a gift from God. If it weren't for him, I may not have become a Christian, and I certainly would not be where I am today without his support. But there came a moment when I had to confront an important question: which relationship mattered most?

I realized I was allowing sin to stand between me and God because I was unwilling to confess it to my husband.

Running has become sacred time with God for me. It is often when I pray- bringing before Him the things that are on my heart for the day. As I run through my neighborhood, I frequently pray for my neighbors and for the specific situations in their lives that I am aware of.

When I am not talking to God, my run becomes all-consuming. When my thoughts center on how hard it feels, how tired I am, how much my muscles hurt, or how much farther I still have to go, those things seem to grow in their influence. They begin to dominate my thoughts and often feel worse than they truly are.

When I align my thoughts with God, however, the run itself seems to fade into the background. What once felt difficult no longer feels overwhelming. When I am in conversation with God, I am not consumed by how many laps remain. My breathing no longer becomes a concern, and the distance seems to pass more quickly.

Our lives work the same way. When we focus on the things of God, other issues, problems, and annoyances begin to fade in priority. They don't always disappear, but they often lose their power over us. When we focus only on the process, it can be difficult to see the finish line. But when we focus on the finish line, the process feels lighter and more manageable. Our walk- or run- with God is no different. Scripture reminds us:

"Then you will win favor and a good name in the sight of God and man. Trust in the LORD with all your heart and lean not on your own understanding; in all your ways submit to him, and he will make your paths straight." (Proverbs 3:4-6, NIV)

We can follow Him reluctantly, or we can choose to cooperate with Him. We can get up on our feet and move forward. It takes energy. It takes effort. And He invites us to respond.

This kind of faith sometimes requires us to give all we have- even when we are exhausted or have not slept the night before. Those moments remind us of our human weakness. At times, they also reveal how poorly prepared we may be, how little we have nourished ourselves.

As we learn to keep pace with Jesus, we also begin to understand what it means to run well alongside the people He places beside us.

Keeping Pace with Others

"Accept the one whose faith is weak, without quarreling over disputable matters." (Romans 14:1, NIV)

Running well with others requires wisdom as much as compassion.

It was exciting when Page decided to run track. I wanted to give her pointers, but most of the time she didn't want to hear them. She already had two coaches and didn't need another- even though I joked that she was lucky to have her own personal one. The reality was that her coaches had forty other athletes to train, while I was simply her mom. It meant a lot to me that she was doing something I had done at her age. She was much faster than I ever was- with longer legs- and while I ran one- and two-mile races, she ran sprints.

We each have our own race to run, and at times, running well means adjusting our pace for others. There are seasons when we run alongside someone because we have something to learn from them, and other times because they need something from us. But here is the caution: we must be careful not to remain at someone else's pace so long that we stop running the race God has set before us. When that happens, dependency can form. They may struggle to move forward without us, and our own run may become hindered. What was meant to help can slowly become a crutch. Discernment is knowing when to slow down for someone- and when obedience requires us to keep moving forward.

There are also times when adjusting our pace can begin to slow us down, and this lesson became clear to me in a very personal way. My husband and I were looking for ways to stay in shape, so for a season we ran together to prepare for a race. After that race was over, we decided to continue running together.

I've learned that God is often more interested in distance- how far we are willing to go- than in how quickly we get there. That understanding has shaped the way I think about running with Him. I had been running with Bob for several months, but I began to feel the need to run on my own because I deeply missed that time with God and the things He teaches me while I run. So I decided to go off on my own.

I began to notice a few practical differences between running alone and running with my husband. When I run by myself, I go in the morning. When we run together, it is usually in the afternoon, because mornings are too busy for him.

When we ran together, our pace was different from when I ran alone. God has made him differently than me; beyond the obvious differences between men and women, he also has a good six inches on me. That naturally gives him a much longer stride than mine.

Because I'm competitive, I pushed myself to keep up with him. But in increasing my stride, I used more energy and lost the ability to go the distance. Stated more clearly, I could run farther at my own pace than at Bob's pace.

Time together is always a gift in the middle of busy schedules. But I began to realize that running with my husband was costing me the quiet space where God often met me. When I ran with him, that intimacy wasn't there. No matter how much I wanted it to be the same, it never quite was. I've never been able to fully explain why. We were focused on pace and breathing- or sometimes too out of breath to talk at all. I was still running, still moving forward, but now Bob was beside me, and the experience was different.

God also creates special relationships between us and other believers.

In the early church, as described in Acts, believers lived as family, and we are called to view one another the same way. It matters that we keep pace with those closest to us. We need to maintain our own pace- sometimes running with them, sometimes running ahead of them, and sometimes falling behind- but always staying close. This is especially true with our spouse and our children. If we are not near them, we cannot be present when they need us, and they cannot be present when we need them. Staying close matters.

Running with others is a gift- but it should never replace the quiet places where God meets us personally.

Sometimes this is extremely difficult, especially when it involves a spouse or a child. There are moments when we feel ourselves moving forward in our walk with God while those closest to us seem to be standing still- or barely moving at all. In those moments, the temptation can be to keep running and leave them behind. After all, Jesus did call His disciples to leave everything and follow Him.

But for most of us, I don't believe Jesus is asking us to abandon the people He has entrusted to us. This can feel contradictory to some of His teachings, including His words about leaving father, mother, sister, brother, or child for the sake of the Kingdom. Too often, I believe these passages are misunderstood or misapplied to justify leaving a marriage or a family. And while it is undeniably difficult when we are unequally yoked, we must be careful to seek God's will rather than acting out of frustration or impatience. Instead of running away to pursue our own spiritual momentum, perhaps God intends to use the growth He is doing in us to help lift others up. When we run ahead without discernment, we can unintentionally leave those we love feeling farther behind rather than strengthened.

I've learned that encouragement doesn't always come loudly- sometimes it comes quietly, simply through presence. One neighbor in particular often sits on his back porch in the mornings, reading the paper as I run past. He doesn't cheer me on, but I know he cares. He has reminded me to drink water and not to overdo it. Some mornings, he has already gone inside before I finish my run. I imagine that if he knew I needed encouragement that day, he would offer it- but he doesn't always know. And that isn't intentional. Maybe on one of those mornings, he was carrying the weight of the recent loss of his father.

The experience of being let down by others is not unfamiliar, and Scripture speaks to it honestly. Joseph remained in prison even after helping Pharaoh's chief cupbearer. He specifically asked to be remembered once the cupbearer was restored to his position, yet two full years passed before he finally recalled what Joseph had done for him. So often, we look to others to be there for us, and they fall short. That is never the case with God.

"Therefore encourage one another and build each other up, just as in fact you are doing." (1 Thessalonians 5:11, NIV)

* * *

Reflection & Prayer

1. What most often pulls my focus away from Jesus and begins to set my pace instead of His?
2. In what areas of my life am I tempted to run at someone else's pace rather than the one God has set for me?
3. Are there relationships in my life that strengthen my walk with God—and are there any that unintentionally crowd out the quiet places where He meets me?
4. When God invites me to slow down, speed up, or adjust my

direction, how do I usually respond?

5. What would it look like for me to intentionally keep Jesus in sight throughout my day?

Lord, teach me to keep my eyes fixed on You. Help me trust Your pace when I want to rush ahead or fall behind. Give me wisdom to walk faithfully with others without losing the path You have set before me. Align my heart with Yours, my steps with Your Spirit, and my life with Your will. Amen.

* * *

4

Running Together - Encouragement, Discipleship, and Legacy

"How, then, can they call on the one they have not believed in? And how can they believe in the one of whom they have not heard? And how can they hear without someone preaching to them? And how can anyone preach unless they are sent? As it is written: 'How beautiful are the feet of those who bring good news!'" (Romans 10:14-15, NIV)

But this race of faith is not just about running in the company of Jesus or alongside those we already know.

Encouraging Others to Run

Running alongside others is not always easy, but it is part of why God leaves us in the race. Our faith journey does not end at salvation; it continues so that we can walk with others as they learn to run. As we do, we must move with wisdom and love, attentive not only to their race, but to our own as well.

We must be grounded enough in our own walk with God to encourage others without losing our footing ourselves. At the same time, we need to be certain we are leading them in the direction God desires- not simply the direction that feels comfortable to us.

Witnessing to different people in the same way can be ineffective- and at times, even harmful. Some people need to be led gently and slowly down the path, while others may need a more direct and honest approach. Often, these differences reflect variations in personality, background, and spiritual readiness.

Discernment matters, because not everyone is running from the same starting line.

We must be attentive to whether the Holy Spirit is already working in their lives and opening a door for us. That can be difficult to discern, which is why we must remain prayerful about the friendships God has placed in our lives.

Scripture reminds us of both our readiness and our restraint:

"But in your hearts revere Christ as Lord. Always be prepared to give an answer to everyone who asks you to give the reason for the hope that you have. But do this with gentleness and respect." (1 Peter 3:15, NIV)

We cannot effectively encourage others unless we are willing to run the race ourselves. Before inviting others to run alongside us, we must first be willing to get out there and run.

Sometimes you may be called to walk with someone if you sense God's leading. This distinction is important to understand. There is a fine but necessary line between allowing someone- who may not truly be seeking to run the race- to hinder our own progress, and slowing down to encourage someone who genuinely desires to run.

Running the Relay — Faith That Carries Forward

"One generation commends your works to another; they tell of your mighty acts." (Psalm 145:4, NIV)

What does it mean to run a relay? A relay is not just about you; it involves others. In any relay- whether running or swimming- we take over where the person before us has left off. They pass us the baton, and we are responsible for taking it and running with it. There is a spiritual component to this as well.

This is what Psalm 145:4 points us toward- faith that doesn't stop with one generation, but is shared, modeled, and carried forward.

I have often thought of this as carrying the torch of my family, passed down from my mom. What feels like a baton in my hands now was formed by God over time- it was not something I always had. I wasn't raised going to church, and it wasn't until later in life that my mom and stepdad came to know the Lord- around the same season my husband led me to Christ. As she and the other matriarchs of our family have since passed, the torch has been entrusted to me- not as a burden, but as a responsibility- one that calls me to be intentional about what I impart to the next generation.

That has caused me to ask important questions: What do I want to leave my children and grandchildren spiritually? What kind of spiritual legacy will I pass on to them?

My mom and stepdad modeled a faith that was active, sacrificial, and lived out daily. They left a legacy of service to those less fortunate than we were, serving for years in the mission field- first spending seven years in Haiti drilling wells, and then another seven years in Honduras caring for ten orphaned children. Their faith was not just something they believed; it was something they lived.

In this season, my husband also carries a responsibility of leadership, shaped by the legacy he received from his father- a legacy marked by faithful service in the church and on mission trips. Together, we are running our leg of the race with what God has entrusted to us.

But I want to pause here, because I know this is not everyone's story.

Not everyone was handed a baton by godly parents or raised in a home where faith was modeled well. Some of us came to faith later in life. Some of us learned what faith looked like by watching others from the outside before stepping into the race ourselves. And some of us didn't receive a baton at all- we are the ones God asked to pick it up for the very first time.

That does not make your race less meaningful. Scripture is filled with people who did not inherit a spiritual legacy but were chosen by God to start one. Your obedience still matters. Your faithfulness still counts. The legacy you are building is no less valuable because it did not begin early or come easily.

Ultimately, God is the One who holds the baton first and places it in our hands- no matter how or when our race begins.

For you, the baton may not have come from a parent. It may have come through a mentor or a spiritual leader in your life. Or perhaps you are beginning this legacy for your family, relying solely on the leading of God. In truth, that is what all of us must do anyway- because even though we are running a relay, our leg of the race will not look exactly like the one before us. We may have a different stride and a different stretch to run.

How do we discern what our leg of the race is meant to be? We must rely on God to show us the path He has set before us.

It is important to look to the foundations of faith laid by those who have gone before us- whether someone close to us, like my mom, or the pillars of faith we encounter in Scripture. Their lives offer guidance and encouragement as we seek to understand what our own race is meant to look like.

The amazing and beautiful part is that Scripture doesn't only show us triumphant finishes. It also shows us injuries, obstacles, and wrong turns along the way. We don't have to beat ourselves up when we fail or fall, because we can see that they did too and despite those things, God was still able to use them. It is a beautiful story of redemption.

It's easy to gloss over familiar words. We hear the words *redeem* and *redemption* often in church, and sometimes we lose sight of what they truly mean.

Here are some of the definitions of *redeem*:

- To buy back or repurchase
- To free from what distresses or harms, such as captivity by payment of ransom, or to help overcome something detrimental
- To release from blame or debt; to clear
- To change for the better; to reform
- To make good or fulfill

Do you see that? Even our failures and falls can be used. And even if we drop the baton, it can become an opportunity for another to pick it up.

My own leg of the race became clear during one of the hardest moments of my life. When my mom passed away, I entered a season of depression. I was already in a difficult place spiritually, and I was separated from the community that would normally help encourage me through it. But when I finally began to emerge from that place, I realized it was time to take up my baton.

God had been shaping my calling in ways I didn't fully recognize at the time. During the years my parents served as missionaries, we visited them both individually and as a family. Those trips weren't vacations; they were opportunities to serve and help others.

One year, we visited during Thanksgiving- a season usually centered on family and food. Instead of focusing on what we would eat, we chose to focus on serving others.

My parents were deeply committed to a particular village in Honduras. Before we left, we collected donations so that when we arrived, we could purchase essentials these families didn't have- rice, beans, and other basic needs. We gathered those supplies and delivered them as a tangible expression of God's love.

Serving others through missions- often in foreign countries- has become a meaningful part of our family's faith journey.

Missions may not be your passion- and that's okay. God calls each of us to serve in different ways. You may support others through generosity that helps meet practical needs. You may be gifted medically, offering care and healing. Or you may have business skills that help people- locally or abroad- build sustainable income to support their families.

Our callings will not all look the same. Each of us is given a unique path to follow, even as we remain connected to one another. Some runs are long and steady, others short and demanding, but each requires faithfulness. Learning how God has asked us to run takes time and trust. In the next chapter, we'll look at how He reveals that path.

* * *

Reflection & Prayer

1. Who has God placed in my life right now that I am called to encourage, walk alongside, or invest in spiritually?
2. In what ways have others shaped my faith journey, and what kind of spiritual legacy am I building for those who come after me?
3. Am I willing to adjust my pace—slowing down or stepping forward—when God invites me to serve someone else?

Faith invites reflection—but it also calls for response.

1. Where might I be relying too heavily on people to meet needs that only God can truly fill?

2. What path has God set before me in this season, and how can I walk it faithfully for His glory?

Lord, thank You for placing people in my life and for placing me in the lives of others. Help me encourage without controlling, serve without replacing You, and love without losing sight of Your lead. Teach me to walk faithfully with those You entrust to me, always pointing them to You—not myself. May my life reflect a legacy of faith that honors You and draws others closer to Your truth. Amen.

* * *

* * *

5

The Course - Purpose, Calling, and Assignment

"In their hearts humans plan their course, but the LORD establishes their steps." (Proverbs 16:9, NIV)

Running Your Assigned Course

While faith is carried forward through others, each of us must still learn to run the course God has personally set before us.

Many times, I do not want to run. It feels easier to stay comfortable or simply move on with my day. Sometimes I even find the motivation to get out there, but I drag myself through the run, wanting to quit before I finish the distance I planned- the course I set before myself.

But when I am done, I feel so much better. My blood is pumping, my body is moving, my lungs are full, and my muscles are warm. After that, I can't sit still.

Sometimes we hear God clearly and still want to deny what we have heard. Other times, we ask Him to speak but are not truly listening for His voice.

One morning while I was running, I noticed someone I didn't

recognize running as well. We weren't running together- she was looping the small inner circle of the neighborhood, while I was running the full perimeter. I caught myself wondering, *Why does she get to run the shorter distance, while I have to go all the way around?*

There have been other times when I've seen neighbors running, and they make it look effortless- even when they're running the same full perimeter I am. One of them makes it look like a breeze. Another neighbor once commented that he looked like a gazelle when he ran. We've all seen images of gazelles in Africa fleeing from a lion; they seem to glide through the air.

We do the same thing in our spiritual walk. If we're honest, most of us have asked God why things seem easier for someone else. But here's the truth: He has set the course before us exactly as He intends.

It occurred to me that this was the first time I had ever seen her running there. Why would I expect her to run the same distance I was running? It's the same with a new Christian. Sometimes God builds our faith in small increments; other times, He grows it through larger steps.

I also noticed she was wearing some kind of brace. Maybe she was running a shorter distance- but she was doing it with an injury, or in spite of one.

Shouldn't I have cheered for her instead? If I were dealing with the same injury she had, would I even be out there running at all?

We can't compare our race to anyone else's. Their course wasn't designed for us, and ours wasn't designed for them. God shapes each of us differently so that He can use our lives- and our stories- in exactly the way He knows is needed.

God not only gives us unique gifts, but also distinct passions, and He uses those together in different ways. My passions have included youth and foreign missions, and more recently, Freedom- which we'll explore later. Not everyone is called to work with teenagers, and I understand that- because sometimes I didn't even like my own- but I always loved them. In the same way, not everyone feels called to serve in a third-world country; some are called to serve faithfully in places like a local food bank.

Scripture reminds us that God does not design us all the same way: *"But one and the same Spirit works all these things, distributing to each one individually as He wills... Now you are the body of Christ, and each one of you is a part of it."* (1 Corinthians 12:11, 27, NIV). God has set each of us in the body exactly as He pleased. No part is unnecessary, and no calling is insignificant. When we compare our race to someone else's, we risk missing the purpose God designed specifically for us.

Running prepares us for more than physical endurance- it trains us for obedience. If we are going to follow God where He calls us, we must be willing to prepare for what that calling requires. In many ways, following God is like being called into the military.

After all, we are called to be part of God's army. I'm reminded of the children's song, *"I'm in the Lord's Army,"* which carries a simple but serious truth. When someone joins any military organization, preparation is essential. Much of that preparation involves rigorous physical training, because those in charge understand what will be required in the field.

If a recruit were to enter the field of battle unprepared, it would likely result in injury- or worse. In our walk of faith, we are also called onto fields of battle. Many of those battles are spiritual, but some are physical as well. We may be called to serve on the mission field in Africa. Can you imagine stepping into that calling without being physically prepared for the rigors it entails? I can't imagine anything worse than being fully surrendered and ready to go for God's purpose, only to find ourselves unable to go because of a limitation we could have prepared for.

Just as David couldn't fight Goliath wearing Saul's armor, and Paul and Peter carried the same message to different people, we must focus on the specific call God has for our lives- not what we see others doing.

Choosing the Long and Narrow Road

Most days when I am running, I go a few miles. One morning, I was really struggling with God- not just about my run, but about life in general. Things were hard. We were struggling financially, still trying to recover from a blow to our business several years earlier.

We had returned to church, we were serving, and we had dedicated our business to God. That dedication hadn't happened at the beginning, because when we started the business, we were in a desert season and not seeking Him. Knowing that, we made a conscious decision to give it fully to God. Still, I wasn't just struggling with my run- I was struggling with my hope, my faith, and my joy.

But I knew from past desert seasons that pulling away from God wouldn't make things any better. In fact, it would only make them worse. I was determined to pursue joy despite my circumstances. So as I ran that morning, I kept praying and turning it all over to God. I listened to worship music as usual, choosing songs like *"Desperate"* and *"Hard-Fought Hallelujah,"* because that was exactly how I felt.

About five minutes into my run, my AirPods died.

In the quiet that followed, I began praying and listening. I tried to count my blessings, yet I still wrestled with why we continued to struggle financially. Why did it feel like a constant roller coaster? In my frustration, I even questioned whether this was the result of disobedience or something generational, and I prayed that anything not from God would be broken in the name of Jesus.

As I continued on, God began to redirect my thoughts. The miles passed almost unnoticed. When I thought I was finished and heading home, God said, *"Take the long way."* I didn't want to, and it didn't make sense- but I obeyed.

After taking the longer route, I assumed I was finally on my way home. Then He said it again: "Take the long way."

Again, God? Why? I had already gone farther than usual—why more?

Take the long way.

"God, what are You trying to show me here?" As I reflected, I realized that while I am comfortable sharing my faith on the mission field and helping believers grow, I often struggle to initiate conversations about faith in everyday life with those who don't yet know Him.

The longer route I was running began to mirror the longer work God was doing in me. He showed me that I needed that extended path- time and space to prepare me for the work He has called me to right here. In some ways, He was still growing areas of my faith.

For a long time, I assumed that sharing faith came more naturally to some than to others- that it was a calling reserved for those with a particular gifting. Over time, however, God reshaped my understanding. I now know that all believers are called to share their faith, even though it may look different from person to person.

So why do so many hesitate? In our culture, faith is often met with resistance. In the name of tolerance, people of faith are frequently dismissed—especially when our beliefs don't align with prevailing cultural values. At times, it feels safer to stay quiet, particularly when we see how harsh the backlash can be against those who speak openly about their faith.

For me, that hesitation has often been shaped by my own wiring and past—by introversion and by wounds connected to rejection—making obedience feel costly even when the call is clear. And even when faith is held and expressed with love, it is not always welcomed.

Lord, I come to You now and ask that You would help me be bold in my faith. Place opportunities before me, and give me the courage to respond each time You do. Work in me so that my life points others to

Christ. Help me become all that You created me to be, in the way You have uniquely shaped me to live and serve.

Show me what obedience looks like in this season, and help me step boldly into the calling You have placed on my life. Give me the platform You desire for me, and fill me with Your Holy Spirit until I overflow- not from my own strength or resources, but from You alone. Engage my heart so deeply with Your presence that I reflect You, as Moses did. Even if You must shelter me and cover me with Your hand, I want to experience Your glory so that I can help others experience it too.

Sometimes obedience doesn't come with clarity- only the next step. And often, that next step asks us to trust God beyond what feels comfortable or familiar.

The long, narrow, and winding road may not be easy. In fact, that's part of the point. But when we stay connected to God, He helps us through- and makes the journey worth it. The experiences we have along the way, the person we become as we walk with Him, and the destination He leads us toward are worth every step.

We are called to trust the promises He has given us through His Word and through His Spirit- the hope, the joy, and the peace that surpass all understanding. When we experience those gifts here on earth, they are small glimpses of what awaits us in heaven. And heaven is eternal.

Even when the road here feels long and winding, it is nothing compared to eternity. Lord, give us glimpses of what eternity looks and feels like, so we have the strength to keep moving forward on the long, narrow road of this life.

Over time, the course God sets before us may shift. We can become complacent, and once we see God work in one area, He often desires to show us His faithfulness in another. He invites our faith to keep growing.

When we sense that pull, we sometimes try to satisfy it through other means, drifting back toward worldly things- especially when we think we've figured out our relationship with God. But faith is not meant to stagnate. God grows it by inviting us into new steps of obedience, often before we feel ready.

God grows our faith through invitation, not stagnation. When He calls us to deeper faith, He often does so through specific steps of obedience. Over time, those steps can become part of our rhythm and routine. But once faith settles into habit, God may invite us forward again- stretching us in new ways so our trust in Him continues to grow.

Even as our faith grows, our pace remains personal. God shapes each of us uniquely. While there are people we will run alongside throughout our lives- some briefly, others repeatedly, like our spouse or our children-we are still responsible for running our own race at the pace God sets for us. We each carry distinct gifts, talents, and callings. Every race unfolds in its own way, even though the destination is the same.

This principle is lived out in practical ways. If my calling includes writing, and my husband tries to run that same race by forcing himself into it, he would struggle- not because he lacks value or faith, but because that course was never designed for him. God has wired us with intention. When we try to run someone else's race, we become ineffective- not only in our own calling, but in theirs as well.

We are called to come alongside others in their walk of faith. Sometimes that means slowing down to walk with someone who is new to faith or returning after time away. Other times, it means quickening our pace to walk with someone who stretches and challenges us to grow. And at times, it means stopping altogether to help lift someone who has stumbled and fallen. These moments are not optional- they are essential. But we must be careful not to become so entangled in someone else's race that we lose sight of our own, or we risk becoming ineffective in what God is calling us to do.

God has something He wants to accomplish specifically through each of us and through the race set before us. It may look very different from what we hoped for or expected, and it may not resemble the path we see others taking- but it is intentional, purposeful, and designed by Him.

Passion for following God can sometimes turn into impatience. We sense His call, but we want to move before the timing is right. Or we feel a stirring of purpose without clear direction and begin filling in the gaps ourselves. When impatience leads the way, we risk stepping ahead of God rather than walking with Him.

When Bob and I first began to sense God's call, our desire to serve Him grew quickly. We prayed for direction, but when clarity didn't come right away, we started making plans of our own. Because some of our most meaningful experiences had been on the mission field, we assumed that meant we were called to serve overseas.

That path didn't open for us, and while the reasons made sense, the waiting was frustrating. Over time, God clarified that our callings- though connected- were distinct. We support and participate in one another's calling, but they are uniquely shaped, and neither requires serving on the mission field to be faithful.

I want to run the course set before me with confidence, trusting God to guide and direct every step. I cannot do that on my own- I need His presence beside me, leading the way. Even when I am confident I am running the right course, God often uses unexpected detours to shape me along the way.

And as long as I stay attentive to His lead, every step- even the detours- becomes part of the course He designed for my good and His glory.

* * *

Reflection & Prayer

1. Where am I most tempted to compare my course to someone else's, and how does that affect my joy or faithfulness?
2. What has God clearly placed in front of me to do right now, even if it feels harder or longer than I expected?
3. Are there areas where I have resisted God's direction because the path feels inconvenient, uncertain, or uncomfortable?
4. How has God used past detours, delays, or struggles to shape me for my current calling?
5. If I trusted God fully with the course He has set for me, what might need to change in my attitude, expectations, or obedience?

Father God, thank You for designing my race with intention and purpose. Help me trust the course You have set, even when I don't understand it. Guard my heart from comparison and impatience, and teach me to walk faithfully in the calling You have given me today. I surrender my plans to You and ask for courage to follow where You lead. Amen.

* * *

* * *

6

Detours, Obstacles, and Course Correction

"Trust in the LORD with all your heart and lean not on your own understanding; in all your ways submit to him, and he will make your paths straight." (Proverbs 3:5-6, NIV)

Even when we are running in obedience, the path God leads us down is not always the one we expect.

Sometimes in our walk of faith, we reach a point where the path turns in a direction we didn't anticipate. We may believe the Spirit has given us direction, yet the crossroads before us don't seem to lead there at all. There may be multiple options- or only one- and none of them feel right. The way forward can feel confusing, even contradictory.

When I first walked to the river, part of my route took me through the parking lot near the boat ramp. Some days it was manageable, but other days it felt chaotic and unsafe. Boats and trailers moved in and out, tides shifted the current, and not everyone navigating the ramp knew what they were doing. Even with only a few boats, the experience felt stressful and unpredictable.

It wasn't until later that I realized there was another way. One day, on my walk back home, I went around a building and discovered a sidewalk that led safely toward the river without ever stepping into the parking lot. I had never considered that route because it felt like the wrong direction. But what seemed out of the way was actually the safest and most direct path.

God's path for us can feel the same way. Sometimes what looks like a detour- or even a step in the wrong direction- is actually the way that protects us, prepares us, or allows us to see something we would have missed otherwise. Detours rarely feel purposeful in the moment, but they often become the places where God does His deepest work in us.

In moments like these, it's easy to wonder whether the detour is the result of something we did wrong- rather than a path God is intentionally using.

There are also times when the path doesn't feel redirected-it feels blocked. Not slowed, not altered, just stopped. One day, I ran down to the boat ramp, looking forward to resting by the water before starting the 2.5-mile walk home. As I approached, I saw sheriff's vehicles and caution tape blocking the entire area. No one was allowed through. I had to turn around and head back the way I came, disappointed and frustrated.

At times, God limits how far we can go in a single day. Even when it feels unfinished or disappointing, that limitation may be part of His preparation for what comes next.

We tend to rush toward whatever comes next. As a Coast Guard saying puts it, we're always looking to the "next next." While that mindset may serve certain roles well, it does not serve our walk with God. We hurry forward, but God does not move at our pace. He values the process, because the process has purpose.

A clear example of the difference between God's perspective and ours comes from my husband and me. He is a big-picture thinker, able to envision what something could become years down the road. I tend to focus on details- taking a goal and working out the steps to get there.

That contrast reminds me of a football game. A kicker fixes his eyes on the goalposts and sends the ball flying, rarely thinking about the space in between. A running back, however, must focus on every step-watching for gaps, adjusting to resistance, and responding moment by moment. On the sidelines, the coach sees the entire field at once. God is our coach. We may only see the next few steps, but He sees the whole field and knows exactly how each moment is shaping us for the finish.

This lesson showed up again for me on my run to the park. Part of that route requires me to begin by heading in a direction that doesn't make sense at first. It feels counter intuitive, yet it ultimately leads me exactly where I need to go.

Some days, I don't make it all the way and have to try again another time. Those moments build persistence. God uses them intentionally-not as setbacks, but as preparation. They strengthen the endurance, faith, and resolve we need to finish the race He has set before us.

"If you refuse to take up your cross and follow me, you are not worthy of being mine. If you cling to your life, you will lose it; but if you give up your life for me, you will find it." (Matthew 10:38-39, NLT)

One of the hardest examples from my own life came during a season when our family was still young. We were living in a house we had built and made our own. I had painted murals in the children's rooms, and the home held deep meaning for me. After my husband was out of work for six months, we began to struggle financially. He accepted a position in Nashville, and although we later decided not to move, our house was already under contract, and we had to sell it.

Leaving that home was one of the hardest things I had ever done. God taught me many lessons through that season- lessons I couldn't fully see at the time.

The real estate market was still strong, and when we sold the house, we were able to purchase a more modest home and had savings for the first time. Within a year, we were approached with a business opportunity that required having cash on hand to sustain the startup period. Had we not sold that house, as painful as it was, we would not have been able to step into that opportunity.

What felt like loss at the time was actually God's provision at work.

When we push through and persist, we begin to understand what it means to be faithful. Scripture doesn't say, "Well done, good servant." It says, "Well done, good and faithful servant."

Faithfulness requires perseverance- continuing forward even when the road is blocked, redirected, or seems to lead the wrong way. We seek the Holy Spirit's guidance and strength, and we keep going.

I often run around the perimeter of my neighborhood. In the Florida summer, the heat can be relentless. Evenings are slightly cooler, but after a full day, I'm often tired and have to push myself just to start.

Our neighborhood is newer, built on what was once an orange grove, which means there are no large trees and very little shade. As the sun rises over the houses, the light becomes so intense that I have to lower my head, even with sunglasses on.

Our walk with God can feel the same way. Sometimes the light of the Son feels overwhelming- not because it is harsh, but because it exposes what has been hidden.

Like stepping from a dark room into sudden light, our eyes need time to adjust. We may want to turn away, but instead we must allow His light to shine on us, even when it is uncomfortable.

Transformation requires staying present in the light.

We may also stumble along the way. One morning, I was running toward the river, planning to rest and spend quiet time with God once I arrived. With the river in sight and less than a quarter mile to go, I fell- hard. My hands and knees were scraped, I was bleeding, and the impact knocked the wind out of me.

Cars passed by, but no one seemed to notice. In that moment, I had a choice. I could call my husband to pick me up. I could turn around and walk home. Or I could press on.

I chose to keep going. I was sore and bleeding, but I was close- and I wasn't willing to give up those moments with God. When I reached the dock, I watched the sunrise, saw the water moving with the tide, and lifted my voice in worship. I sang praises to my King, because He is always worthy.

Jesus endured far more than scraped knees and exhaustion. With a bruised, beaten, and bleeding body, He pressed on to the cross because it was worth it. He saw beyond the pain to the redemption it would bring. He saw us standing before the Father, hearing, "Well done, good and faithful servant." And He chose obedience- for you and for me.

And I choose to do the same. I will press on through obstacles. I will walk when the path feels wrong. I will try again when the road is closed. I will trust Him through detours and delays until the day I see my Savior face to face and hear, "Well done, my good and faithful servant."

* * *

Reflection & Prayer

1. Where have you experienced a detour in life that didn't make sense at the time?
2. How do you typically respond when your plans are interrupted or your path feels blocked?
3. What might God be teaching you in a season where progress feels slow or unclear?
4. What would it look like to trust God's direction, even when it leads somewhere unexpected?
5. What is one area where I need to stop resisting a detour and instead

ask God what He is teaching me through it?

God, I confess that I often want the shortest and clearest path. Help me trust You when the way feels uncertain. Give me patience in detours, faith in delays, and courage to follow where You lead. Teach me to remain faithful when progress feels slow, and to believe that You are at work even when I cannot see it. Amen.

* * *

7

Injuries, Wounds, and Freedom

"But he was pierced for our transgressions, he was crushed for our iniquities; the punishment that brought us peace was on him, and by his wounds we are healed." (Isaiah 53:5, NIV)

Injuries

When we're running, it doesn't have to be pretty. Many times, we limp toward the finish line in our race of faith- but we keep going. God can turn our ugliest seasons into places of great beauty. It is in my weakness that He is glorified; it is there that His strength becomes visible.

Over time, the way we run begins to change. I had been running all the way around the lake for at least a month, and then one day I couldn't make it. Sometimes it's easier when we first begin, because we place no pressure on ourselves. We have no expectations- we simply run, do our best, and trust that God is pleased.

But after we've been running for a while, expectations creep in. That's often when we are most vulnerable. We push too hard. We shift our focus from *why* we are running to what we think we *should* be doing.

When we turn our focus back to Jesus in those moments, He honors that.

Case in point: less than a week earlier, I had cut three minutes off my overall time. My mistake was starting to time myself. On the very next run, I was right back to my old pace.

Just when you start to get comfortable and settle into a routine- when you're confident you can finish- the unexpected happens.

I run a two-mile wooded course. For weeks, I thought about everything along the path that could trip me up. I even prepared for preventable obstacles like uneven ground or pulled muscles.

And then one day, it happened.

There it was- a snake.

I dislike snakes more than almost anything. In our walk with God, Satan will sometimes step directly into our path- especially when our confidence begins to grow. But Scripture reminds us that *"You, dear children, are from God and have overcome them, because the one who is in you is greater than the one who is in the world."* (1 John 4:4, NIV). When we stand firm, the enemy retreats.

Then it happened again- except this time, the snake didn't move. Its head was raised, ready to strike.

As I got closer, I realized it wasn't a snake at all. It was just a branch.

Sometimes the obstacle is Satan. Sometimes it's our imagination. Fear of what *might* be ahead can paralyze us just as effectively as a real threat. But when God guides us and fills us with His Spirit, we learn to recognize distractions for what they are—and keep running.

Injuries are part of running- but wounds are what happen when those injuries go untreated.

Wound Care

One distinction that has helped me is understanding that scars are not wounds. Wounds may leave scars, but scars are healed. They no longer bleed, ache, or remain infected.

Some wounds take longer to heal than others, and some leave visible marks while others do not. Healing is not always obvious from the outside, but it is real nonetheless.

Scars can remind us of where we've been and strengthen us moving forward- but we must be careful not to reopen what God has already healed. When wounds are reopened, they can become infected and cause deeper damage, making healing more difficult the next time.

I want to be a good mother to my children, yet I still make poor decisions at times. We fail one another- often more than we'd like to admit. It is only through God's redeeming power that any good comes from our lives. Even with His help, we continue to live in a broken world that bears the weight of abuse, infidelity, divorce, and so much more.

Freedom

There came a time in my life when I realized I needed freedom in my run- freedom from chasing times and distances, and from tracking my runs simply to prove that I had done them. I had to ask myself why I needed validation at all, and why it mattered who saw it.

When my focus shifted back to simply running with God- without performance, comparison, or applause- I found freedom. What mattered was not who saw it or how it was measured, but that God knew. He used that time exactly as He intended.

Through the blood of Jesus, we are brought from death to life. The grave is opened. We are no longer dead. Yet many believers never move beyond that moment. They are alive, but still bound. The door stands open, but the grave clothes remain.

Like Lazarus in John 11, we may be standing outside the tomb-breathing, moving, alive- yet still wrapped in what once held us captive. Until those bindings are removed, freedom remains limited and movement restricted.

Too many Christians live this way: saved, but stuck. Alive, but weighed down. When life still feels heavy and joy feels distant, it becomes difficult to live fully- or to share hope with others.

Salvation is essential- we cannot experience freedom without it. But freedom is what allows us to walk in step with the Holy Spirit and live effectively. Without freedom, we survive- but we do not thrive.

Freedom is not a one-time moment- it is a journey we must continue walking. Breaking free from the past does not mean the fight is over. We are called to guard what God has given us as we move forward.

The Israelites' story in Exodus illustrates this clearly. Their slavery ended when they crossed the Red Sea. The Egyptians were defeated and no longer pursuing them. Yet even after undeniable deliverance, they continued to think and live like slaves. They doubted God's provision and even claimed life had been better in Egypt (Exodus 16:3).

They hesitated to step into the land God had promised- not because God was unable or unwilling, but because their mindset had not yet caught up with their freedom. Many never experienced the Promised Land, not as punishment, but as the natural consequence of continuing to live as though they were still bound.

Freedom removes the chains- but it also calls us forward into the race that still lies ahead.

* * *

Reflection & Prayer

1. Where in my life have injuries turned into wounds because I ignored them, minimized them, or tried to push through without healing?
2. Are there areas where I'm living with a wound that God wants me to bring into the light for healing?
3. What fears or imagined threats have distracted me or slowed my pace in this season?
4. Where do I feel "alive in Christ" but still bound—still carrying grave clothes that God wants removed?
5. What is one step of freedom God is asking me to take right now—an act of obedience, surrender, or honest prayer?

God, thank You for bringing me from death to life and for opening the grave. Show me where I am still holding onto chains that You want to remove. Help me tend to my wounds with honesty and trust, and not reopen what You have already healed. Teach me how to live freely, fully alive, and led by Your Spirit as I continue to run this race with You. Amen.

* * *

Note: Not all churches use the language of "Freedom," but many teach similar biblical principles of healing, repentance, forgiveness, renewal, and walking fully alive in Christ. If you would like to explore these themes more deeply, a list of Scripture passages and recommended resources is included in the appendix.

* * *

8

Running for Your Life - Urgency and Endurance

"For your sake we are in danger of death at all times; we are treated like sheep that are going to be slaughtered." (Romans 8:36, GNT)

Some challenges are harder than others- not just because of their intensity, but because of what they demand from us. The greater the struggle, the greater the opportunity for growth and deeper dependence on God.

It's often assumed that becoming a Christian makes life easier, but many believers would say the opposite is true. Our decisions become more difficult- not because our struggles are greater than those of others, but because we are called to respond in a way that reflects Christ. Scripture even calls us to "count it all joy."

This chapter would not have been possible without the influence of a dear friend, Mike Storter. When I first began writing, Mike was in a battle for his life as he and his family faced his second recurrence of leukemia. At the time of his diagnosis, Mike was given two weeks or less to live.

Each Sunday, as he prayed before our welcome time, he gave

a powerful testimony to our church. This chapter had remained unwritten until that season, and Mike became my inspiration to finish it.

Mike has since gone to be with Jesus.

As I watched Mike walk through this season, I wrestled with a difficult question: how do you count it all joy when death is imminent? Mike lived each day knowing he would leave behind his wife and children. While most of us understand that life is fragile, we often live as though tomorrow is guaranteed. Mike did not have that luxury.

How does someone handle that reality, and what can we learn from it? From the start, Mike and Laura gave God permission to do through their lives- and through this situation- whatever would bring Him honor and glory. They committed themselves to glorifying God, regardless of the outcome.

In the depths of it all, they lived out that commitment. When many would have questioned whether God still loved them, Mike and Laura demonstrated a deeper trust in the love of Christ- as if God had pulled back the curtain and given them a glimpse of eternity. That perspective created an urgency to ensure that every person they encountered heard about Christ. Doctors and nurses- people they may never have met otherwise- became witnesses to a faith shaped by hope rather than fear.

Mike and Laura were more concerned with the eternal lives of those around them than with preserving Mike's own life. Mike was prepared for eternity- and he wanted to make sure others were as well.

Mike lived a truly sacrificial life. He willingly surrendered the outcome of his healing to God, which placed him before people he may never have encountered otherwise. Through this, he modeled a way of living that consistently put the needs of others before his own. This testimony extended beyond the hospital and became a defining influence within their home.

The Storters also used this time to prepare their children in ways they may not have anticipated. They created tangible reminders of Mike's love, including videos for important moments when he would be especially missed.

But this kind of situation also creates an opportunity to prepare a family in less tangible ways. When we are running for our lives- and fully aware of it- we are given the chance not only to witness to those who do not know Christ, but also to strengthen the faith of those who already do. We can pass on lessons that are often learned only through hardship.

At a young age, the Storter girls learned what it looks like to trust God in the face of extreme difficulty- because that is what their parents consistently modeled for them.

Through it all, they were also taught to keep their focus on sharing Jesus with a lost world- not as an obligation, but as a natural overflow of hope.

Courage in the face of suffering is not limited by age.

Sweet Natalie Harrell- the kind of joyful second-grade cheerleader you can't help but smile at. In just a few short months, she went from being a healthy, active little girl to being diagnosed with a life-threatening brain tumor.

Yet as you read through their journal and saw the family in church, what stood out most was not fear, but courage. Natalie's positive attitude in the midst of suffering, along with her family's steady strength in God, became a powerful testimony to those around them. Through treatment and uncertainty, they reflected a faith that did not waver with circumstances.

Stories like Natalie's have a way of re-centering our hearts. They remind us that suffering does not negate faith- and that gratitude, trust, and compassion can exist even in the hardest circumstances.

For those walking a similar path without the hope of Christ, stories like this should move us to share the hope we have found in Him.

Jesus said, *"I have come that they may have life, and have it more abundantly."* (John 10:10b, NKJV). This does not mean we will be spared from struggle or trial- we will all face them. But it does mean we can experience a deeper joy, even in hardship.

As I have faced challenges in my own life, I have often been able to consider them with joy because God has consistently shown Himself faithful. Those difficulties were not wasted; they were part of the refining process that drew me closer to Him.

That is what I ultimately desire. If that has not been your experience yet, it may be because God has not revealed the purpose to you- at least not yet. Sometimes we must look closely and dig deeply to recognize His faithfulness. Other times, we may not fully understand until we reach heaven.

But if you look back, you will almost certainly find evidence of God's faithfulness woven throughout your life.

Scripture instructs us: *"But you, keep your head in all situations, endure hardship, do the work of an evangelist, discharge all the duties of your ministry."* (2 Timothy 4:5, NIV).

God allows us to walk through circumstances that can be deeply challenging- sometimes overwhelmingly so. Yet it is often in those very moments that His faithfulness is revealed, even when we cannot immediately see how good could come from them.

When we find ourselves running for our lives and the road feels urgent, we are called to endure- not in our own strength, but with our eyes fixed on eternity. God is faithful. He always has been, and He always will be. And our endurance is never wasted.

* * *

Reflection & Prayer

1. When have you been most aware that life is fragile and time is not guaranteed?
2. What does "counting it all joy" look like for you when life does not go as planned?
3. How does remembering that this life is not the end shape the way you live, love, and respond to others?
4. Who in your life may need the hope of Christ, even if you feel unprepared or uncomfortable sharing it?
5. What is one way God may be inviting you to live more intentionally in light of eternity right now?

Lord, teach me to care for what You have entrusted to me—body, heart, and spirit. Help me to prepare well, not in my own strength, but through daily dependence on You. Remind me to seek Your Word and Your presence before I grow weary. Shape my habits so I can run faithfully and finish strong. Amen.

* * *

* * *

9

Running Away from God

"So do not throw away your confidence; it will be richly rewarded. You need to persevere so that when you have done the will of God, you will receive what he has promised. For in just a very little while, 'He who is coming will come and will not delay.'" (Hebrews 10:35-37, NIV)

One morning, Bob and I started out walking together. It was shortly after I had begun writing, during a season when life felt especially heavy. I was frustrated with how things were unfolding. I believed God was directing my path, but that belief did not make the journey any less painful. I was tired. I was weary.

That morning, I was exercising out of habit, frustration, and a need to release anxiety. I didn't want to run with God or focus on Him. I wanted to sit in my frustration, not hear words of inspiration. As Bob and I walked, I poured out everything to him- my situation, my struggle with God, and my questions about why He was allowing these things to happen. I cried. I was in the valley.

Bob later told me that when I finished, he didn't know what to say. He didn't know how to help me. After we finished walking, I went on to run.

As I ran, I asked God not to pour into me the way He had been. It wasn't that I didn't want Him there, but His words no longer felt encouraging, and I didn't want to hear them. I pushed His thoughts out of my mind for as long as I could.

Near the end of my run, I became both physically and emotionally exhausted. I couldn't fight anymore.

That was when God poured into me in an incredible way. When I finally stopped resisting, He began to heal.

Within an hour, my attitude changed- not because my circumstances had shifted, but because God changed my perspective. I was given a glimpse of His purposes and plans, even though I still could not fully understand what He was doing. Even now, I cannot say I see it clearly. Some wounds take time to heal.

But when I loosened my grip, God met me with comfort and peace.

There are times in our lives when we run from God.

This does not always look like abandoning belief; sometimes it looks like emotional distance, silence, or choosing not to engage because trust has been wounded.

There are many reasons this happens. I shared some examples in the previous chapter- injuries, obstacles, and pain that cut so deeply we begin to doubt. We question whether God truly wants what is best for us.

During that time, I had been surrounded by tragedy. A young wife and mother lost her husband in a car accident, leaving her sons without their father. One of my daughter's eleven-year-old friends lost a stepfather to suicide. Miscarriages, cancer diagnoses, the death of a child, the end of a marriage- these things happen around us, and sooner or later, they happen to us.

Pain, loss, and confusion are often the places where the enemy attempts to pull us away from trust. He uses them to make us want to stop running altogether. We may feel the urge to pull away from

God- to be angry with Him, to question why He allowed these things to happen.

Those emotions are natural. For some, this distance lasts days or months; for others, it stretches into years.

But do not allow Satan to pull you away from a loving Father. God can carry us through these moments. Cry out to Him when you feel He is silent. Cry out when you cannot understand why the pain was allowed. Cry, break down, and be honest. When we release those emotions and surrender the pain, God is able to begin His healing work in us.

Often, we try to handle pain in our own strength. I know I do. Taking control and fixing things feels natural to me, even when surrender would be the better path. Yet there are moments when the only way forward is to release our grip and allow God to take control- to trust Him to do what we cannot and redeem what feels broken.

Satan's goal is to knock us off course. He does not want us fulfilling God's purpose for our lives. He does not want us to experience joy, and he certainly does not want us to share that joy with others- because when we do, they may be drawn closer to God themselves.

Jesus makes the contrast clear: *"The thief's purpose is to steal and kill and destroy. My purpose is to give them a rich and satisfying life."* (John 10:10, NLT).

***

Reflection & Prayer

1. When have I noticed myself pulling away from God instead of running toward Him?
2. What emotions or circumstances most often tempt me to create

distance from Him?

3. Where am I trying to fix things in my own strength rather than surrendering control to God?
4. How has God met me with grace and peace when I finally stopped resisting Him?
5. What would it look like for me to stay present with God, even when His work in me feels uncomfortable?

God, I confess that there are times when I pull away from You instead of running toward You. When pain, confusion, or fear overwhelms me, draw me back into Your presence. Help me release control, trust Your heart, and allow You to heal what I cannot fix. Remind me that You are a loving Father who never abandons me, even when I struggle to believe it. Amen.

* * *

10

Finishing Strong

"I have fought the good fight, I have finished the race, I have kept the faith. Now there is in store for me the crown of righteousness, which the Lord, the righteous Judge, will award to me on that day—and not only to me, but also to all who have longed for his appearing."
(2 Timothy 4:7-8, NIV)

Paul wasn't talking about speed- he was talking about faithfulness to the end.

With the exception of when I ran track in high school, my running has rarely been preparation for a specific race. But there was a season in my life when that changed.

Bob and I had been participating in shorter obstacle runs like Warrior Dash and Mud Run- mostly for fun. Then Bob decided to take it to a whole other level- or as our church likes to say, a *"hole notha level."* If you know, you know. He and a group of friends signed up for Tough Mudder, a grueling five-to-ten-plus-mile obstacle course designed to test physical strength, mental grit, and teamwork rather than speed.

Heavily inspired by British Special Forces training, it features more than seventeen military-style obstacles- ice pits, barbed wire crawls, and even electroshock- designed to build camaraderie and push participants beyond their comfort zones. After he completed it one year, I decided- or perhaps he convinced me- to do it the following year. Looking back, that race was unlike anything I had ever done, and it mirrors our walk of faith more closely than I realized at the time.

There were moments during the race when I completely failed at the task in front of me- like the monkey bars, which defeated me more than once. There were times when I was injured, times when I fell and had to get back up, and moments when I questioned whether I could keep going. Each obstacle demanded something different: strength, balance, endurance, or help from someone else. And still, the race continued.

Reaching the finish line was incredibly satisfying, but before I could cross it, I had to endure one final obstacle- electric shock treatment. It was unpleasant, humbling, and painful, and afterward I carried the bruises to prove it.

Yet crossing that finish line made every obstacle worth it- much like the day we will cross the final finish line of our faith and step into eternity with Christ.

Running With the Finish in Mind

When we run, it is natural to set a goal for ourselves- a finish line. We don't usually run aimlessly until we are exhausted; instead, we choose a specific place to stop or a certain amount of time to run. We begin with that destination in mind, whether we can see it or not.

As the run goes on, our thoughts often drift toward the finish line. Sometimes it is because we are tired and ready to be done. Other times, it is because the end feels far away and we are longing to reach it.

Our walk of faith is much the same. There is a finish line, but it is not one we set for ourselves- God does. We do not know the day or the hour when Christ will return or when we will be called home.

Even so, we are called to run toward that finish line as if it were just around the corner, giving everything we have along the way.

I once had someone describe a job to me this way: "I want you to run this race as if it is a 100-meter dash, not a two-mile run." What he was asking of me was simple but demanding- to give my best every day, in every step.

He wanted me to put my full effort into the work set before me, not holding anything back, but running with urgency and intention until the finish.

If you approach a race believing it is a two-mile run, you will set a pace that feels sustainable and comfortable. But if the starting gun goes off and the other runners explode forward in a sprint, it becomes clear very quickly that this is not the race you thought it was.

In that moment, you must decide whether to cling to your original pace- or adjust to the reality unfolding before you.

In the same way, we must be willing to adjust our pace in our Christian walk. Our first and constant goal must be to become more like Christ. As God reveals new truth, new responsibility, or a new season, we cannot remain committed to a pace that no longer fits His calling. Faithfulness requires attentiveness- and a willingness to move when He says move.

Many times when I am running, I picture Jesus running beside me. As I get closer to finishing, I sometimes imagine Him moving out ahead of me- or even waiting at the very spot I have chosen as my finish line.

But we must be ready for that picture to change. When it does, we have to rely on Him for the strength and encouragement to keep going, trusting that He knows exactly where the true finish line lies.

Let's face it- we are creatures of habit. We settle into routines that feel familiar and comfortable, and before long, we stop paying attention to whether we are still where God wants us to be. Comfort can quietly replace calling if we are not careful, and what once required faith can slowly become something we do out of habit rather than obedience.

We must make sure we remain in a place of service or ministry because God is leading us there- not simply because it feels familiar or safe. Staying attentive to His direction requires humility and courage, especially when obedience asks us to move beyond what we know or where we feel most comfortable.

It is important to examine why we remain where we are serving. Are we still there because God has called us to that place, or because it has become comfortable and familiar?

Following God faithfully sometimes means stepping away from what feels safe in order to remain aligned with His will.

Sometimes we reach what we think is the finish line only to realize we still had more to give. One morning, I set my finish line as my house. When I arrived, I realized I was not tired yet, so I kept running and finished farther down the street. Only afterward did I realize I had misjudged my finish line and had to turn back.

We do not want that to happen in our walk of faith. Many times, we grow attached to our earthly homes and routines, and as we run toward them, we unconsciously set an easy pace. But our true destination is far greater. Our heavenly home is our final finish line, and it deserves our full effort and wholehearted pursuit.

Even when we give our best, failure is still a part of life. We may pour everything we have into a marriage and still watch it fall apart. We may give our all as parents, only to see a child choose a path far from Christ. We make commitments we struggle to keep and face outcomes we never wanted. Failure, in one form or another, is part of the human experience.

For a Christian, however, there is only one true failure: not finishing the race having given it our all. We may stumble in many areas of life, but when we stand before Him, what will matter most is that we remained faithful and endured to the end, longing to hear the words, "Well done, good and faithful servant."

We decide at the beginning of our run that we are going to finish the race- and finish it strong. In our walk with God, that decision must be settled in our hearts ahead of time. No matter the circumstances or the struggle, we commit ourselves to running faithfully with Him and giving everything we have until the end.

The mind and will are powerful things. When we set our hearts and minds on finishing the race God has given us, we gain the strength to push through obstacles and endure what feels overwhelming. Even as we grow older, tired, or weak, that settled determination helps carry us forward- trusting that God will supply what we lack as we press on toward home.

At times, God gives us the strength to finish strong through sheer endurance. At other times, He carries us with grace, just as Psalm 91 describes- lifting us up, steadying our steps, and making the journey lighter. There are seasons when it feels as though we are running effortlessly, almost floating along with Him. He keeps pace with us, slowing down or moving ahead as needed- always present, always guiding, always faithful to get us home.

As Christians, we often hear the phrase "looking toward home." We truly do have more to look forward to than the grave- it is not our final destination. Heaven is. Any joy, peace, or happiness we experience here is only a glimpse of what awaits us there.

One day, the race will be over. We will rest in the arms of Christ and spend eternity with Him, and every step taken in faith will have been worth it.

If you have read this book and realized that you are not yet running this race with Christ, I want you to know that the invitation is still open. God is not waiting for you to be stronger, faster, or more prepared—He is simply waiting for your yes. I have included something at the end of this book for you, because the most important step in any race is the decision to begin.

* * *

Reflection & Prayer

1. What does "finishing strong" look like in my current season of life- not someday, but now? Where have I grown comfortable instead of remaining attentive to God's calling?
2. Am I running my race with the urgency of eternity in mind, or at a pace shaped by convenience?
3. In what areas might God be asking me to give a little more- faith, effort, obedience, or trust?
4. How does the hope of heaven change the way I endure today's challenges?

Lord, thank You for calling me to run this race with purpose and hope. Help me keep my eyes fixed on You and my heart set on eternity. When I grow tired or comfortable, renew my strength and my resolve. Teach me to finish well—not in my own power, but through Your grace. I long to hear one day, "Well done, good and faithful servant." Until then, help me run faithfully with You, every step of the way. Amen.

* * *

Your Tomorrow

I have hope in Your tomorrow,
Because my tomorrow just won't do.
I keep trying with my own plans,
Trying to make them work without You.
I set my mind on Your path—
I can't do this on my own.
When I take it out of Your hands,
It feels like I'm walking alone.
I rest my hope in Your promise
That You are always by my side.
Guide my steps toward what You will,
And keep my heart abiding still.
When the path becomes hard,
And I think I can no longer bear,
Help me to know without a doubt
Your faithful love surrounds me there.
Jesus, please walk beside me
Down this path that You have set.
May Your love and gentle guidance
Stay with my every step.

* * *

* * *

Appendix A: If You're Not Yet Running This Race

If you've read this book and realized that what I've described feels unfamiliar—or even unreachable—it may be because you've never experienced a relationship with Jesus. And if that's the case, I want you to know this: you can begin that relationship today.

You may feel unworthy of God, distant from Him, or unsure whether faith is even possible for you. The Bible tells us that God desires a relationship with every one of us—not because we are good enough, but because He is loving and merciful. Scripture also reminds us that all of us fall short and cannot make ourselves right with God on our own.

That is why God made a way.

Jesus, God's own Son, lived a sinless life and willingly took our place. He bore the weight of our sin on the cross so that we could be restored to God without shame or guilt. He did not remain in the grave, but rose again, defeating death and making new life possible—both now and for eternity.

If you believe this, even if you feel unsure or full of questions, you can respond to God right where you are.

You might pray something as simple as this:

God, I want to know You. I believe that Jesus is Your Son and that He gave His life so I could be forgiven and made new. I don't have everything figured out, but I am choosing to trust You and begin this journey with You. Lead me as I learn what it means to

run this race with You. Amen.

If you've prayed this—or even if you're just beginning to wonder—please don't walk this road alone. Seek out a trusted pastor, a Christian friend, or a local church where you can ask questions and grow in your faith. God never intended this race to be run in isolation.

Your journey doesn't end here.

In many ways, it's just beginning.

Appendix B: Freedom - Walking the Race Unbound

Not all churches use the word *Freedom* to describe this part of the Christian journey. Some may call it discipleship, healing, sanctification, or spiritual formation. While the language may differ, the heart is the same: learning how to walk fully alive in Christ, no longer bound by what once held us captive.

Salvation brings us from death to life. Freedom teaches us how to live that life unencumbered.

Many believers experience genuine salvation but continue to struggle with patterns of fear, shame, unforgiveness, insecurity, or hidden wounds. This does not mean their faith is weak or their salvation incomplete—it means there is more healing God desires to do.

Throughout Scripture, we see that God not only rescues His people, but also restores them.

The Israelites were delivered from slavery in Egypt in a single moment, yet it took time for their hearts and minds to catch up with their freedom. Even after the chains were removed, they often thought and lived like slaves. In the same way, many Christians have been set free in Christ, yet still carry beliefs, habits, or wounds formed in bondage.

Jesus addressed this when He said:

"You will know the truth, and the truth will set you free." (John 8:32, NIV)

Freedom is not about striving harder—it is about surrendering deeper.

It often involves:

- Identifying lies we have believed about God, ourselves, or others
- Bringing wounds, sin, and strongholds into the light
- Learning to forgive and receive forgiveness
- Releasing control and inviting the Holy Spirit to heal what we cannot

Freedom is rarely a single moment. It is a process—one that unfolds through prayer, community, truth, and obedience.

If You Want to Explore Freedom Further

If your church offers a Freedom, inner healing, or discipleship pathway, consider stepping into it with openness and humility. These environments are not about exposing weakness, but about creating space for healing and growth.

If your church does not offer a specific Freedom curriculum, you are not without options. God is faithful to meet those who seek Him.

Here are some healthy ways to pursue Freedom:

- Trusted, prayerful community
- Biblically grounded discipleship groups
- Christian counseling with a strong spiritual foundation
- Guided study focused on identity in Christ, forgiveness, and healing

Above all, Freedom begins with a willingness to ask God:

"Is there anything in me that You want to heal, reveal, or remove so I can walk more freely with You?"

He is gentle, faithful, and patient. He does not rush the process—and He never forces it.

A Final Encouragement

Freedom is not a detour from the race—it is part of the preparation.

God does not reveal wounds to shame us, but to heal us. He does not invite us into Freedom to slow us down, but to help us run unhindered.

As Scripture reminds us:

"Let us throw off everything that hinders and the sin that so easily entangles. And let us run with perseverance the race marked out for us." (Hebrews 12:1, NIV)

If God is stirring something in you as you read this, do not ignore it. Respond gently. Take one step. Ask one honest question. Invite Him into one place you've kept guarded.

That is how Freedom begins.

Scripture References

In some instances, Scripture passages have been adapted or paraphrased for devotional clarity and readability.

Acknowledgments

For a long time, this book felt like something God gave just for me- not because it was meant to remain private, but because fear made it feel safer that way. I resisted sharing it, returning to these pages in different seasons while quietly hoping they could remain personal. The hesitation was not about readiness; it was about vulnerability and the risk of being seen. God, in His patience, allowed the distance, the questions, and the delay. In time, He made it clear that obedience would require releasing what I was trying to protect. This book exists because He would not let fear have the final word.

This book was also formed in a desert season- a time when I was not drawing closer to God, but actively trying to pull away. That season was marked by loss, silence, and the absence of the spiritual support I once relied on. Yet it was there, and in the season that followed, that God did a deeper work. Some of what is written here could only have been shaped by walking through the desert and emerging with a faith refined by honesty, freedom, and endurance rather than certainty.

To my husband: thank you for always saying yes. Yes to my ideas, yes to my questions, and yes to the things God has placed on my heart- even when the path was unclear or unpredictable. You have been steady and supportive in ways that mattered deeply, offering reassurance, pride, and presence without requiring explanation or justification. Your belief in me has been a gift I do not take lightly.

To my children- my daughters and son: I am deeply thankful for the relationship I share with each of you. You are all wonderfully different, and I treasure the closeness we have, knowing that such relationships are not automatic or guaranteed. Your love, grace, and acceptance have anchored me more than you know, especially during seasons when my faith was being stretched and reshaped.

To my sons-in-law, and to the families you are building with my daughters, including the gift of grandchildren: thank you for the love, care, and steadiness you bring into our lives. It is a joy to watch the ways you lead, serve, and love faithfully, and I am deeply grateful for the role you play in our family.

I am deeply grateful for one friend who walked closely with me through the final stretch of this process. You believed in me when I hesitated, affirmed that my voice mattered, and reminded me that what God placed in me was worth sharing. Your confidence in this calling helped me find the courage to release it. You know who you are- and I pray you hold the same confidence in what God has clearly placed in you. You are talented, equipped, and called, even if fear of rejection has tried to quiet that truth. I hope my yes encourages yours, one step at a time.

Experiencing Freedom- through my church community and beyond- gave me the courage to step forward in faith rather than retreat in fear. To the people of my church: thank you for creating space for healing, honesty, and growth. You did not rush the process or demand an outcome. You loved, supported, and encouraged obedience, and this book is fruit of that community.

This book is written in loving memory of my mom. Her passing came during that desert season, and the weight of losing her shaped me profoundly. Even in her fight against leukemia, she demonstrated quiet strength, humble faith, and a deep heart for serving others. She lived a life of sacrificial obedience, caring for people without recognition or fanfare. I pray that I have taken the torch she carried and run with it faithfully, honoring the legacy she entrusted to me.

And to the reader: if you find yourself in a season of resistance, grief, or distance from God, know that His faithfulness does not depend on your closeness. My prayer is that these pages remind you that God meets us even in the desert- and that what He forms there is never wasted.

About the Author

Nicole B. Adams writes from her own journey of learning to trust God more deeply through seasons of uncertainty, growth, and surrender. She serves as a facilitator in her church's Freedom ministry and is passionate about walking alongside others as they pursue spiritual healing and deeper intimacy with Christ.

She is actively involved in supporting U.S. Coast Guard families during boot camp, sharing encouragement and devotional reflections for those navigating the unique challenges of that season. With a heart for missions and for meeting people in their hardest moments, Nicole desires to remind believers that faithfulness often looks steady and unseen.

Nicole lives in Florida with her husband, children, and granddaughters, who are her greatest treasure.

www.ingramcontent.com/pod-product-compliance
Lightning Source LLC
LaVergne TN
LVHW090535110826
845146LV00003B/1101